50 Chicken Dishes for Every Occasion

By: Kelly Johnson

Table of Contents

- Roast Chicken with Herbs
- Chicken Alfredo
- Chicken Parmesan
- Grilled Chicken Skewers
- Chicken Tikka Masala
- Lemon Garlic Chicken
- BBQ Chicken Wings
- Chicken Caesar Salad
- Chicken and Rice Casserole
- Chicken Piccata
- Honey Mustard Chicken
- Chicken Marsala
- Chicken Fajitas
- Buffalo Chicken Wraps
- Chicken Pot Pie
- Chicken and Vegetable Stir Fry
- Chicken Enchiladas
- Baked Chicken Thighs
- Chicken Satay
- Chicken Biryani
- Chicken Shawarma
- Chicken Soup
- Crispy Fried Chicken
- Chicken and Broccoli Pasta
- Chicken Quesadillas
- Grilled Chicken Salad
- Stuffed Chicken Breast
- Teriyaki Chicken
- Chicken and Dumplings
- Chicken and Spinach Stuffed Shells
- Spicy Chicken Tenders
- Chicken Schnitzel
- Chicken Cacciatore
- Lemon Chicken Risotto
- Chicken Shawarma Wraps

- Cajun Chicken Pasta
- Chicken Fried Rice
- Chicken and Bacon Ranch Casserole
- Chicken Fettuccine Alfredo
- Chicken and Corn Chowder
- Jerk Chicken
- Chicken Croquettes
- Chicken Burrito Bowls
- Chicken Tortilla Soup
- Parmesan Crusted Chicken
- Sweet and Sour Chicken
- Mediterranean Chicken Salad
- Chicken Chili
- Honey Garlic Chicken
- Chicken Kebabs

Roast Chicken with Herbs

Ingredients:

- 1 whole chicken (about 4-5 lbs)
- 2 tbsp olive oil
- 1 tbsp fresh thyme leaves
- 1 tbsp fresh rosemary leaves
- 1 lemon, halved
- 4 garlic cloves, smashed
- Salt and freshly ground black pepper, to taste
- 1 onion, quartered
- 1 cup chicken broth

Instructions:

1. **Prepare the Chicken:** Preheat the oven to 425°F (220°C). Remove the giblets from the chicken and pat it dry with paper towels.
2. **Season the Chicken:** Rub the chicken with olive oil, thyme, rosemary, salt, and pepper. Stuff the cavity with the lemon halves, garlic cloves, and onion quarters.
3. **Roast the Chicken:** Place the chicken breast side up in a roasting pan. Pour the chicken broth into the pan. Roast the chicken for about 1 hour and 15 minutes, or until the internal temperature reaches 165°F (75°C).
4. **Rest and Serve:** Let the chicken rest for 10 minutes before carving and serving.

Chicken Alfredo

Ingredients:

- 1 lb fettuccine pasta
- 2 tbsp butter
- 2 garlic cloves, minced
- 2 cups heavy cream
- 1 cup grated Parmesan cheese
- 2 cups cooked chicken breast, sliced
- Salt and freshly ground black pepper, to taste
- Fresh parsley, chopped (for garnish)

Instructions:

1. **Cook the Pasta:** Cook the fettuccine according to package instructions. Drain and set aside.
2. **Prepare the Alfredo Sauce:** In a large skillet, melt butter over medium heat. Add garlic and cook for 1 minute. Stir in heavy cream and bring to a simmer. Reduce heat and add Parmesan cheese, stirring until smooth.
3. **Combine the Chicken and Pasta:** Add the sliced chicken to the sauce and cook for another 2-3 minutes until heated through. Season with salt and pepper.
4. **Serve:** Toss the cooked fettuccine with the Alfredo sauce. Garnish with chopped parsley and serve immediately.

Chicken Parmesan

Ingredients:

- 4 boneless, skinless chicken breasts
- 1 cup all-purpose flour
- 2 large eggs, beaten
- 1 cup breadcrumbs
- 1/2 cup grated Parmesan cheese
- 2 cups marinara sauce
- 1 cup shredded mozzarella cheese
- 2 tbsp olive oil
- Fresh basil, chopped (for garnish)

Instructions:

1. **Prep the Chicken:** Preheat the oven to 400°F (200°C). Dredge each chicken breast in flour, dip in beaten eggs, and coat with breadcrumbs mixed with Parmesan cheese.
2. **Cook the Chicken:** Heat olive oil in a skillet over medium heat. Cook the chicken breasts for 4-5 minutes per side, until golden and cooked through. Remove and set aside.
3. **Assemble the Dish:** Place the chicken breasts in a baking dish. Spoon marinara sauce over each breast, then sprinkle with mozzarella cheese.
4. **Bake:** Bake for 15-20 minutes, or until the cheese is melted and bubbly.
5. **Serve:** Garnish with fresh basil and serve with pasta or a side salad.

Grilled Chicken Skewers

Ingredients:

- 2 lbs chicken breast, cut into cubes
- 2 tbsp olive oil
- 1 tbsp lemon juice
- 1 tbsp honey
- 1 tsp ground cumin
- 1 tsp paprika
- 2 garlic cloves, minced
- Salt and freshly ground black pepper, to taste
- Wooden skewers (soaked in water for 30 minutes)

Instructions:

1. **Marinate the Chicken:** In a bowl, whisk together olive oil, lemon juice, honey, cumin, paprika, garlic, salt, and pepper. Add the chicken cubes and marinate for at least 30 minutes.
2. **Prepare the Skewers:** Thread the marinated chicken cubes onto the skewers.
3. **Grill the Chicken:** Preheat the grill to medium-high heat. Grill the skewers for 5-7 minutes per side until the chicken is cooked through.
4. **Serve:** Serve with rice, salad, or a yogurt dipping sauce.

Chicken Tikka Masala

Ingredients:

- 1 lb chicken breast, cubed
- 1 tbsp vegetable oil
- 1 onion, chopped
- 2 garlic cloves, minced
- 1 tbsp ginger, grated
- 2 tbsp garam masala
- 1 tsp ground cumin
- 1 tsp ground coriander
- 1 tsp turmeric
- 1 can (14 oz) diced tomatoes
- 1/2 cup heavy cream
- Salt and freshly ground black pepper, to taste
- Fresh cilantro, chopped (for garnish)

Instructions:

1. **Cook the Chicken:** Heat oil in a large pan over medium heat. Add the chicken and cook until browned, about 5-6 minutes. Remove and set aside.
2. **Prepare the Sauce:** In the same pan, add onion, garlic, and ginger. Cook until the onion is softened. Stir in garam masala, cumin, coriander, and turmeric. Cook for 1 minute.
3. **Simmer the Sauce:** Add diced tomatoes and cook for 10 minutes. Stir in the heavy cream and cooked chicken. Simmer for another 10 minutes until the chicken is fully cooked and the sauce has thickened.
4. **Serve:** Season with salt and pepper. Garnish with fresh cilantro and serve with naan or rice.

Lemon Garlic Chicken

Ingredients:

- 4 chicken breasts
- 2 tbsp olive oil
- 4 garlic cloves, minced
- Zest and juice of 1 lemon
- 1 tsp dried oregano
- Salt and freshly ground black pepper, to taste
- Fresh parsley, chopped (for garnish)

Instructions:

1. **Prepare the Chicken:** Season the chicken breasts with salt, pepper, and oregano.
2. **Cook the Chicken:** Heat olive oil in a skillet over medium-high heat. Add the chicken breasts and cook for 5-6 minutes per side, until golden and cooked through.
3. **Make the Sauce:** In the same pan, add garlic, lemon zest, and lemon juice. Stir and cook for 2 minutes, scraping up any browned bits from the pan.
4. **Serve:** Spoon the sauce over the chicken and garnish with chopped parsley.

BBQ Chicken Wings

Ingredients:

- 2 lbs chicken wings
- 1/2 cup BBQ sauce
- Salt and freshly ground black pepper, to taste
- 1 tbsp olive oil

Instructions:

1. **Prepare the Wings:** Preheat the grill or oven to 400°F (200°C). Toss the chicken wings with olive oil, salt, and pepper.
2. **Grill or Bake:** Grill the wings for 25-30 minutes, or bake for 30-35 minutes, turning occasionally, until crispy and cooked through.
3. **Toss in BBQ Sauce:** Once the wings are cooked, toss them in BBQ sauce and serve immediately.

Chicken Caesar Salad

Ingredients:

- 4 cooked chicken breasts, sliced
- 8 cups Romaine lettuce, chopped
- 1/2 cup Caesar dressing
- 1/4 cup grated Parmesan cheese
- Croutons, for garnish

Instructions:

1. **Prepare the Salad:** In a large bowl, toss the Romaine lettuce with Caesar dressing.
2. **Assemble the Salad:** Arrange the sliced chicken on top of the dressed lettuce. Sprinkle with Parmesan cheese and croutons.
3. **Serve:** Serve immediately as a refreshing and filling meal.

Chicken and Rice Casserole

Ingredients:

- 2 cups cooked chicken, shredded
- 1 1/2 cups cooked rice
- 1 can (10.5 oz) cream of chicken soup
- 1 cup shredded cheddar cheese
- 1/2 cup frozen peas
- Salt and freshly ground black pepper, to taste

Instructions:

1. **Prepare the Casserole:** Preheat the oven to 375°F (190°C). In a large bowl, combine shredded chicken, cooked rice, cream of chicken soup, cheese, and peas. Season with salt and pepper.
2. **Assemble:** Pour the mixture into a greased 9x13-inch baking dish.
3. **Bake:** Bake for 20-25 minutes until hot and bubbly.
4. **Serve:** Let the casserole rest for 5 minutes before serving.

Chicken Piccata

Ingredients:

- 4 boneless, skinless chicken breasts
- 1/2 cup all-purpose flour
- 2 tbsp olive oil
- 1/4 cup dry white wine
- 1/4 cup fresh lemon juice
- 1/4 cup capers, drained
- 1/2 cup chicken broth
- 1/4 cup fresh parsley, chopped
- Salt and freshly ground black pepper, to taste

Instructions:

1. **Prep the Chicken:** Dredge the chicken breasts in flour, shaking off any excess.
2. **Cook the Chicken:** Heat olive oil in a large skillet over medium heat. Cook the chicken breasts for 3-4 minutes per side until golden and cooked through. Remove the chicken from the skillet and set aside.
3. **Make the Sauce:** In the same skillet, add wine, lemon juice, capers, and chicken broth. Bring to a simmer and cook for 5 minutes until the sauce slightly thickens.
4. **Serve:** Return the chicken to the skillet and coat with the sauce. Sprinkle with fresh parsley and serve immediately.

Honey Mustard Chicken

Ingredients:

- 4 boneless, skinless chicken breasts
- 1/4 cup Dijon mustard
- 1/4 cup honey
- 2 tbsp olive oil
- 1 tbsp apple cider vinegar
- Salt and freshly ground black pepper, to taste

Instructions:

1. **Prepare the Sauce:** In a small bowl, whisk together Dijon mustard, honey, olive oil, apple cider vinegar, salt, and pepper.
2. **Cook the Chicken:** Heat olive oil in a skillet over medium-high heat. Cook the chicken breasts for 6-7 minutes per side until golden and cooked through.
3. **Glaze the Chicken:** Brush the honey mustard sauce onto the chicken during the last few minutes of cooking.
4. **Serve:** Serve the chicken with any remaining sauce drizzled on top.

Chicken Marsala

Ingredients:

- 4 boneless, skinless chicken breasts
- 1/2 cup all-purpose flour
- 2 tbsp olive oil
- 1/2 cup Marsala wine
- 1 cup chicken broth
- 8 oz cremini or white mushrooms, sliced
- 2 tbsp butter
- Salt and freshly ground black pepper, to taste
- Fresh parsley, chopped (for garnish)

Instructions:

1. **Prep the Chicken:** Dredge the chicken breasts in flour, shaking off any excess.
2. **Cook the Chicken:** Heat olive oil in a skillet over medium heat. Cook the chicken for 4-5 minutes per side until golden brown. Remove and set aside.
3. **Prepare the Sauce:** In the same skillet, add mushrooms and cook for 3 minutes. Add Marsala wine and chicken broth, scraping the bottom of the pan. Simmer for 5 minutes.
4. **Finish the Dish:** Stir in butter and return the chicken to the skillet. Cook for 5-7 minutes, until the chicken is fully cooked and the sauce thickens.
5. **Serve:** Garnish with fresh parsley and serve with mashed potatoes or pasta.

Chicken Fajitas

Ingredients:

- 4 boneless, skinless chicken breasts, sliced into strips
- 1 onion, sliced
- 1 bell pepper, sliced
- 1 tbsp olive oil
- 2 tsp chili powder
- 1 tsp cumin
- 1 tsp paprika
- 1 lime, juiced
- Salt and freshly ground black pepper, to taste
- Flour tortillas
- Optional toppings: sour cream, guacamole, salsa, shredded cheese

Instructions:

1. **Marinate the Chicken:** In a bowl, combine olive oil, chili powder, cumin, paprika, lime juice, salt, and pepper. Toss the chicken strips in the marinade and let sit for 15-30 minutes.
2. **Cook the Chicken:** Heat olive oil in a skillet over medium-high heat. Cook the chicken strips for 5-6 minutes, until browned and cooked through.
3. **Add Vegetables:** Add the sliced onion and bell pepper to the skillet and cook for an additional 3-4 minutes until tender.
4. **Serve:** Serve the chicken and vegetable mixture in warm flour tortillas with optional toppings.

Buffalo Chicken Wraps

Ingredients:

- 2 cups cooked chicken, shredded
- 1/4 cup buffalo sauce
- 1/4 cup ranch or blue cheese dressing
- 4 large flour tortillas
- 1 cup shredded lettuce
- 1/2 cup shredded carrots
- 1/2 cup diced celery
- Optional: crumbled blue cheese

Instructions:

1. **Prepare the Chicken:** In a bowl, toss the shredded chicken with buffalo sauce and ranch or blue cheese dressing.
2. **Assemble the Wraps:** Place a tortilla on a flat surface. Layer with shredded lettuce, carrots, celery, and buffalo chicken.
3. **Wrap and Serve:** Fold in the sides of the tortilla and roll it up. Serve immediately, with optional blue cheese crumbles.

Chicken Pot Pie

Ingredients:

- 2 cups cooked chicken, diced
- 1 cup frozen mixed vegetables
- 1 can (10.5 oz) cream of chicken soup
- 1/2 cup chicken broth
- 1/2 cup milk
- 1 tsp dried thyme
- 2 pre-made pie crusts
- Salt and freshly ground black pepper, to taste

Instructions:

1. **Prepare the Filling:** In a large bowl, combine cooked chicken, mixed vegetables, cream of chicken soup, chicken broth, milk, thyme, salt, and pepper.
2. **Assemble the Pie:** Roll out one pie crust and fit it into a pie dish. Add the chicken mixture into the pie crust. Top with the second pie crust and trim the excess. Crimp the edges to seal and cut a few slits in the top.
3. **Bake:** Preheat the oven to 375°F (190°C). Bake for 30-35 minutes, until the crust is golden brown.
4. **Serve:** Let the pie cool for 5 minutes before serving.

Chicken and Vegetable Stir Fry

Ingredients:

- 2 chicken breasts, sliced into thin strips
- 1 tbsp vegetable oil
- 1 cup broccoli florets
- 1 bell pepper, sliced
- 1 carrot, julienned
- 1 onion, sliced
- 2 tbsp soy sauce
- 1 tbsp oyster sauce (optional)
- 1 tsp sesame oil
- 1 tbsp cornstarch mixed with 2 tbsp water (optional for thickening)
- Salt and freshly ground black pepper, to taste

Instructions:

1. **Cook the Chicken:** Heat vegetable oil in a large pan or wok over medium-high heat. Add the chicken and cook for 5-6 minutes, until browned and cooked through.
2. **Stir Fry the Vegetables:** Add the vegetables to the pan and stir fry for 3-4 minutes until tender-crisp.
3. **Add the Sauce:** Stir in soy sauce, oyster sauce, sesame oil, and cornstarch mixture (if using). Cook for 2-3 minutes until the sauce thickens.
4. **Serve:** Season with salt and pepper to taste. Serve with rice or noodles.

Chicken Enchiladas

Ingredients:

- 2 cups cooked chicken, shredded
- 1 can (10 oz) enchilada sauce
- 1 cup shredded cheese (cheddar or Mexican blend)
- 8 corn tortillas
- 1/2 cup chopped onion
- 1/4 cup sour cream (optional)
- Fresh cilantro, chopped (for garnish)

Instructions:

1. **Preheat the Oven:** Preheat the oven to 375°F (190°C).
2. **Assemble the Enchiladas:** Lightly warm the tortillas to make them pliable. In each tortilla, add shredded chicken, a little onion, and a spoonful of enchilada sauce. Roll up and place in a baking dish.
3. **Top with Sauce and Cheese:** Pour remaining enchilada sauce over the rolled tortillas and sprinkle with shredded cheese.
4. **Bake:** Bake for 20 minutes, or until the cheese is melted and bubbly.
5. **Serve:** Garnish with sour cream and cilantro.

Baked Chicken Thighs

Ingredients:

- 6 bone-in, skin-on chicken thighs
- 2 tbsp olive oil
- 1 tbsp paprika
- 1 tsp garlic powder
- 1 tsp onion powder
- 1 tsp dried thyme
- Salt and freshly ground black pepper, to taste

Instructions:

1. **Preheat the Oven:** Preheat the oven to 425°F (220°C).
2. **Prepare the Chicken:** Pat the chicken thighs dry with paper towels. Rub with olive oil, paprika, garlic powder, onion powder, thyme, salt, and pepper.
3. **Bake the Chicken:** Place the chicken thighs on a baking sheet and bake for 30-35 minutes, until the skin is crispy and the internal temperature reaches 165°F (75°C).
4. **Serve:** Let the chicken rest for 5 minutes before serving.

Chicken Satay

Ingredients:

- 4 boneless, skinless chicken breasts, cut into strips
- 1/4 cup soy sauce
- 2 tbsp peanut butter
- 2 tbsp honey
- 1 tbsp lime juice
- 1 tsp ground ginger
- 2 garlic cloves, minced
- 1 tbsp sesame oil
- 1/4 tsp red pepper flakes (optional)
- Wooden skewers (soaked in water for 30 minutes)

Instructions:

1. **Marinate the Chicken:** In a bowl, whisk together soy sauce, peanut butter, honey, lime juice, ginger, garlic, sesame oil, and red pepper flakes (if using). Add the chicken strips to the marinade and refrigerate for at least 30 minutes.
2. **Grill the Chicken:** Thread the marinated chicken strips onto soaked wooden skewers. Preheat a grill or grill pan over medium heat. Grill the chicken for 3-4 minutes on each side until cooked through.
3. **Serve:** Serve the chicken satay with a side of peanut dipping sauce or a cucumber salad.

Chicken Biryani

Ingredients:

- 2 cups basmati rice
- 2 tbsp vegetable oil
- 1 onion, sliced
- 3 garlic cloves, minced
- 1 tbsp grated ginger
- 2 chicken breasts, cut into pieces
- 2 tbsp curry powder
- 1/2 tsp ground turmeric
- 1/2 tsp cumin
- 1/2 tsp ground cinnamon
- 1/2 tsp cardamom
- 1/2 cup yogurt
- 1/2 cup chicken broth
- 1/4 cup chopped cilantro
- Salt to taste

Instructions:

1. **Prepare the Rice:** Cook basmati rice according to package instructions. Set aside.
2. **Cook the Chicken:** Heat oil in a large skillet over medium heat. Add onions and cook until softened. Add garlic, ginger, and chicken pieces, and cook until the chicken is browned.
3. **Add Spices and Yogurt:** Stir in curry powder, turmeric, cumin, cinnamon, and cardamom. Cook for 2 minutes before adding yogurt and chicken broth. Simmer for 5 minutes.
4. **Combine and Serve:** Layer the cooked rice with the chicken mixture. Cover and cook for 10 minutes on low heat. Garnish with cilantro and serve.

Chicken Shawarma

Ingredients:

- 4 boneless, skinless chicken thighs
- 2 tbsp olive oil
- 1 tbsp ground cumin
- 1 tbsp ground coriander
- 1 tsp ground paprika
- 1 tsp ground turmeric
- 1/2 tsp cinnamon
- 2 garlic cloves, minced
- Juice of 1 lemon
- Salt and pepper, to taste
- Pita or flatbread, for serving

Instructions:

1. **Marinate the Chicken:** In a bowl, combine olive oil, cumin, coriander, paprika, turmeric, cinnamon, garlic, lemon juice, salt, and pepper. Coat the chicken thighs in the marinade and refrigerate for at least 1 hour.
2. **Cook the Chicken:** Preheat a grill or skillet over medium-high heat. Grill or cook the chicken for 5-7 minutes per side until cooked through and charred.
3. **Serve:** Slice the chicken and serve with pita or flatbread and your favorite toppings, such as lettuce, tomatoes, cucumbers, and tahini sauce.

Chicken Soup

Ingredients:

- 2 tbsp olive oil
- 1 onion, chopped
- 2 carrots, sliced
- 2 celery stalks, chopped
- 2 garlic cloves, minced
- 6 cups chicken broth
- 2 cups cooked chicken, shredded
- 1 cup egg noodles or any pasta
- Salt and pepper, to taste
- Fresh parsley, chopped (for garnish)

Instructions:

1. **Cook the Vegetables:** In a large pot, heat olive oil over medium heat. Add the onion, carrots, celery, and garlic. Cook until the vegetables are softened.
2. **Make the Soup:** Add chicken broth, shredded chicken, and noodles to the pot. Bring to a boil, then reduce to a simmer and cook for 10-15 minutes until the noodles are tender.
3. **Serve:** Season with salt and pepper to taste. Garnish with fresh parsley and serve hot.

Crispy Fried Chicken

Ingredients:

- 4 bone-in, skin-on chicken pieces
- 2 cups buttermilk
- 2 cups all-purpose flour
- 1 tsp garlic powder
- 1 tsp onion powder
- 1 tsp paprika
- Salt and pepper, to taste
- Vegetable oil, for frying

Instructions:

1. **Marinate the Chicken:** Place the chicken pieces in a bowl and cover with buttermilk. Let it marinate in the refrigerator for at least 2 hours or overnight.
2. **Prepare the Coating:** In a shallow dish, mix flour, garlic powder, onion powder, paprika, salt, and pepper.
3. **Fry the Chicken:** Heat vegetable oil in a large pan over medium-high heat. Dredge the marinated chicken in the flour mixture, coating it evenly. Fry the chicken for 8-10 minutes per side until golden brown and cooked through.
4. **Serve:** Drain the fried chicken on a paper towel-lined plate and serve hot.

Chicken and Broccoli Pasta

Ingredients:

- 2 boneless, skinless chicken breasts, cubed
- 2 tbsp olive oil
- 1/2 cup chicken broth
- 1 cup heavy cream
- 1 cup grated Parmesan cheese
- 2 cups broccoli florets
- 8 oz pasta (penne, fusilli, or spaghetti)
- Salt and pepper, to taste

Instructions:

1. **Cook the Pasta:** Cook pasta according to package instructions. In the last 3 minutes of cooking, add the broccoli florets to the pot to blanch them.
2. **Cook the Chicken:** While the pasta cooks, heat olive oil in a skillet over medium heat. Add the chicken cubes and cook until browned and cooked through. Remove the chicken from the skillet and set aside.
3. **Make the Sauce:** In the same skillet, add chicken broth and heavy cream. Bring to a simmer and cook for 3-4 minutes. Stir in Parmesan cheese, and season with salt and pepper.
4. **Combine and Serve:** Add the cooked pasta, broccoli, and chicken to the skillet. Toss everything to combine and serve hot.

Chicken Quesadillas

Ingredients:

- 2 cooked chicken breasts, shredded
- 1 cup shredded cheese (cheddar, Monterey Jack, or a mix)
- 1/2 cup salsa
- 4 flour tortillas
- 1 tbsp olive oil
- Sour cream and guacamole, for serving

Instructions:

1. **Prepare the Filling:** In a bowl, combine shredded chicken, cheese, and salsa.
2. **Assemble the Quesadillas:** Place a tortilla on a flat surface and spread the chicken mixture evenly on one half. Top with another tortilla.
3. **Cook the Quesadillas:** Heat olive oil in a skillet over medium heat. Cook the quesadillas for 3-4 minutes per side until golden brown and crispy.
4. **Serve:** Slice into wedges and serve with sour cream and guacamole.

Grilled Chicken Salad

Ingredients:

- 4 boneless, skinless chicken breasts
- 1 tbsp olive oil
- Salt and pepper, to taste
- 6 cups mixed greens (lettuce, spinach, arugula, etc.)
- 1/2 cup cherry tomatoes, halved
- 1/2 cucumber, sliced
- 1/4 cup red onion, thinly sliced
- 1/4 cup balsamic vinaigrette

Instructions:

1. **Grill the Chicken:** Preheat a grill or grill pan. Rub the chicken breasts with olive oil and season with salt and pepper. Grill for 5-7 minutes per side until cooked through.
2. **Assemble the Salad:** In a large bowl, toss the mixed greens, tomatoes, cucumber, and red onion.
3. **Serve:** Slice the grilled chicken and place on top of the salad. Drizzle with balsamic vinaigrette and serve.

Stuffed Chicken Breast

Ingredients:

- 4 boneless, skinless chicken breasts
- 1 cup spinach, chopped
- 1/2 cup cream cheese, softened
- 1/4 cup grated Parmesan cheese
- 1 garlic clove, minced
- 1 tbsp olive oil
- Salt and pepper, to taste

Instructions:

1. **Prepare the Filling:** In a bowl, combine spinach, cream cheese, Parmesan cheese, and garlic.
2. **Stuff the Chicken:** Using a sharp knife, create a pocket in each chicken breast. Stuff the chicken with the spinach mixture.
3. **Cook the Chicken:** Heat olive oil in a skillet over medium heat. Season the chicken with salt and pepper, then cook for 6-7 minutes per side until golden brown and the chicken is cooked through.
4. **Serve:** Let the chicken rest for 5 minutes before serving.

Teriyaki Chicken

Ingredients:

- 4 boneless, skinless chicken breasts
- 1/2 cup soy sauce
- 1/4 cup honey
- 2 tbsp rice vinegar
- 2 tbsp sesame oil
- 2 garlic cloves, minced
- 1-inch piece of ginger, grated
- 1 tbsp cornstarch (optional, for thickening)
- Sesame seeds and chopped green onions, for garnish

Instructions:

1. **Make the Teriyaki Sauce:** In a small saucepan, combine soy sauce, honey, rice vinegar, sesame oil, garlic, and ginger. Bring to a simmer over medium heat and cook for 5 minutes. If you prefer a thicker sauce, mix 1 tablespoon of cornstarch with 2 tablespoons of water and add it to the sauce, simmering for an additional 2-3 minutes.
2. **Cook the Chicken:** Grill or pan-fry the chicken breasts over medium heat for 6-7 minutes per side until fully cooked.
3. **Glaze the Chicken:** Brush the chicken with the teriyaki sauce during the last minute of cooking.
4. **Serve:** Garnish with sesame seeds and chopped green onions before serving.

Chicken and Dumplings

Ingredients:

- 2 tbsp butter
- 1 onion, chopped
- 2 carrots, diced
- 2 celery stalks, chopped
- 3 garlic cloves, minced
- 4 cups chicken broth
- 2 cups cooked chicken, shredded
- 1/2 cup heavy cream
- 1 1/2 cups all-purpose flour
- 1 tbsp baking powder
- 1 tsp salt
- 1/2 tsp black pepper
- 1/4 cup parsley, chopped

Instructions:

1. **Prepare the Soup:** In a large pot, melt butter over medium heat. Add onion, carrots, celery, and garlic. Cook until softened, about 5 minutes. Add chicken broth and bring to a boil.
2. **Make the Dumplings:** In a bowl, combine flour, baking powder, salt, and pepper. Add 1/2 cup heavy cream and stir to form a dough.
3. **Add Chicken and Dumplings:** Stir the shredded chicken into the broth. Drop spoonfuls of the dumpling dough into the simmering broth. Cover and cook for 10-15 minutes, until dumplings are cooked through.
4. **Serve:** Garnish with fresh parsley and serve hot.

Chicken and Spinach Stuffed Shells

Ingredients:

- 12 large pasta shells
- 2 cups cooked chicken, shredded
- 1 cup spinach, chopped
- 1/2 cup ricotta cheese
- 1 cup shredded mozzarella cheese
- 1/2 cup Parmesan cheese
- 1 jar marinara sauce
- 1 tbsp olive oil
- Salt and pepper, to taste

Instructions:

1. **Cook the Shells:** Boil the pasta shells according to package instructions. Drain and set aside.
2. **Prepare the Filling:** In a bowl, combine shredded chicken, spinach, ricotta cheese, mozzarella cheese, Parmesan, salt, and pepper.
3. **Stuff the Shells:** Fill each cooked shell with the chicken and spinach mixture.
4. **Bake the Dish:** Preheat oven to 375°F (190°C). Spread marinara sauce in a baking dish, then arrange the stuffed shells in the dish. Cover with more sauce and mozzarella cheese, and bake for 20 minutes, until bubbly.
5. **Serve:** Serve hot with a sprinkle of Parmesan.

Spicy Chicken Tenders

Ingredients:

- 1 lb chicken tenders
- 1 cup buttermilk
- 1 tsp paprika
- 1 tsp cayenne pepper
- 1/2 tsp garlic powder
- 1/2 tsp onion powder
- 1 cup breadcrumbs
- 1/4 cup flour
- 1/2 tsp salt
- 1/4 tsp black pepper
- Oil for frying

Instructions:

1. **Marinate the Chicken:** Soak the chicken tenders in buttermilk for at least 30 minutes to tenderize.
2. **Prepare the Breading:** In a shallow dish, combine paprika, cayenne pepper, garlic powder, onion powder, breadcrumbs, flour, salt, and pepper.
3. **Bread the Chicken:** Dredge each chicken tender in the breadcrumb mixture, coating well.
4. **Fry the Chicken:** Heat oil in a skillet over medium heat. Fry the tenders for 4-5 minutes per side until crispy and golden.
5. **Serve:** Serve hot with dipping sauce, such as ranch or hot sauce.

Chicken Schnitzel

Ingredients:

- 4 boneless, skinless chicken breasts
- 1 cup all-purpose flour
- 2 large eggs, beaten
- 1 1/2 cups breadcrumbs
- 1 tsp salt
- 1/2 tsp black pepper
- 2 tbsp olive oil
- Lemon wedges, for serving

Instructions:

1. **Prepare the Chicken:** Pound the chicken breasts to an even thickness, about 1/2 inch thick.
2. **Breading:** Dredge the chicken in flour, dip into the beaten eggs, and coat with breadcrumbs.
3. **Cook the Chicken:** Heat olive oil in a large skillet over medium-high heat. Fry the chicken for 4-5 minutes on each side until golden and crispy.
4. **Serve:** Serve with lemon wedges for squeezing over the schnitzel.

Chicken Cacciatore

Ingredients:

- 4 bone-in chicken thighs
- 2 tbsp olive oil
- 1 onion, chopped
- 2 garlic cloves, minced
- 1 bell pepper, sliced
- 1 cup diced tomatoes
- 1/2 cup chicken broth
- 1/2 cup red wine (optional)
- 1 tsp dried oregano
- 1 tsp dried basil
- Salt and pepper, to taste
- Fresh parsley, for garnish

Instructions:

1. **Brown the Chicken:** In a large skillet, heat olive oil over medium heat. Brown the chicken thighs for 4-5 minutes on each side, then remove from the skillet.
2. **Cook the Vegetables:** In the same skillet, add onion, garlic, and bell pepper. Cook until softened, about 5 minutes.
3. **Make the Sauce:** Add diced tomatoes, chicken broth, red wine (if using), oregano, basil, salt, and pepper. Stir to combine.
4. **Simmer the Chicken:** Return the chicken to the skillet and cover. Simmer for 30-40 minutes, until the chicken is fully cooked.
5. **Serve:** Garnish with fresh parsley and serve with pasta or rice.

Lemon Chicken Risotto

Ingredients:

- 2 boneless, skinless chicken breasts, cubed
- 1 tbsp olive oil
- 1 cup Arborio rice
- 1 onion, chopped
- 2 garlic cloves, minced
- 4 cups chicken broth
- 1/2 cup white wine (optional)
- Juice and zest of 1 lemon
- 1/2 cup grated Parmesan cheese
- Salt and pepper, to taste

Instructions:

1. **Cook the Chicken:** In a skillet, heat olive oil over medium heat. Add the cubed chicken and cook for 5-7 minutes until browned. Remove and set aside.
2. **Make the Risotto:** In the same pan, cook the onion and garlic for 2 minutes. Add Arborio rice and stir for 1-2 minutes.
3. **Add the Liquids:** Gradually add chicken broth, 1/2 cup at a time, stirring constantly. Once absorbed, add more broth. Continue until the rice is cooked and creamy (about 20 minutes).
4. **Finish the Dish:** Stir in lemon juice, zest, Parmesan cheese, and the cooked chicken. Season with salt and pepper to taste.
5. **Serve:** Serve hot with extra Parmesan on top.

Chicken Shawarma Wraps

Ingredients:

- 4 boneless, skinless chicken thighs
- 1 tbsp olive oil
- 1 tbsp ground cumin
- 1 tbsp ground coriander
- 1 tsp turmeric
- 1 tsp paprika
- 1/2 tsp cinnamon
- 2 garlic cloves, minced
- 1/4 cup lemon juice
- Salt and pepper, to taste
- 4 pita or flatbreads
- Toppings: cucumber, tomatoes, onions, tahini sauce, or yogurt

Instructions:

1. **Marinate the Chicken:** In a bowl, combine olive oil, cumin, coriander, turmeric, paprika, cinnamon, garlic, lemon juice, salt, and pepper. Coat the chicken thighs in the marinade and refrigerate for at least 1 hour.
2. **Cook the Chicken:** Grill or cook the marinated chicken thighs in a skillet for 6-7 minutes per side until fully cooked.
3. **Assemble the Wraps:** Slice the cooked chicken and place it in pita or flatbreads. Add your choice of toppings, such as cucumber, tomatoes, onions, tahini sauce, or yogurt.
4. **Serve:** Roll up the wraps and serve immediately.

Cajun Chicken Pasta

Ingredients:

- 2 boneless, skinless chicken breasts
- 2 tbsp Cajun seasoning
- 1 tbsp olive oil
- 1 onion, chopped
- 2 garlic cloves, minced
- 1 bell pepper, sliced
- 1 cup heavy cream
- 1/2 cup chicken broth
- 8 oz pasta (penne or fettuccine)
- 1/2 cup grated Parmesan cheese
- Salt and pepper, to taste

Instructions:

1. **Prepare the Chicken:** Coat the chicken breasts with Cajun seasoning.
2. **Cook the Chicken:** In a skillet, heat olive oil over medium heat and cook the chicken for 6-7 minutes on each side, until fully cooked. Slice the chicken thinly.
3. **Cook the Pasta:** While the chicken is cooking, boil pasta according to package directions.
4. **Make the Sauce:** In the same skillet, cook onion, garlic, and bell pepper until softened. Add heavy cream and chicken broth. Simmer for 5 minutes.
5. **Finish the Dish:** Add cooked pasta to the sauce, then stir in Parmesan cheese and sliced chicken. Toss to coat and serve.

Chicken Fried Rice

Ingredients:

- 2 cups cooked rice (preferably day-old)
- 2 boneless, skinless chicken breasts, diced
- 2 tbsp soy sauce
- 1 tbsp sesame oil
- 1 onion, chopped
- 1 cup frozen peas and carrots
- 2 garlic cloves, minced
- 2 eggs, scrambled
- 2 green onions, sliced
- Salt and pepper, to taste

Instructions:

1. **Cook the Chicken:** Heat sesame oil in a large skillet or wok over medium-high heat. Add the diced chicken and cook for 5-7 minutes until fully cooked. Remove from the skillet and set aside.
2. **Cook the Vegetables:** In the same skillet, add onion, garlic, and peas and carrots. Stir-fry for 3-4 minutes until softened.
3. **Make the Fried Rice:** Add the cooked rice to the skillet and stir well. Add soy sauce, and salt, and pepper. Stir to combine.
4. **Add Eggs and Chicken:** Push the rice to the side and scramble the eggs in the same skillet. Once cooked, mix them into the rice along with the cooked chicken.
5. **Serve:** Garnish with sliced green onions and serve hot.

Chicken and Bacon Ranch Casserole

Ingredients:

- 2 cups cooked chicken, shredded
- 6 slices bacon, cooked and crumbled
- 1 packet ranch seasoning mix
- 1 cup sour cream
- 1 cup shredded cheddar cheese
- 1/2 cup milk
- 8 oz elbow macaroni or pasta of choice
- Salt and pepper, to taste

Instructions:

1. **Cook the Pasta:** Boil the pasta according to package instructions. Drain and set aside.
2. **Prepare the Sauce:** In a large bowl, mix sour cream, ranch seasoning, milk, and half of the shredded cheddar cheese. Stir to combine.
3. **Combine the Ingredients:** In a large casserole dish, combine cooked chicken, crumbled bacon, cooked pasta, and the ranch mixture. Stir well to coat.
4. **Bake the Casserole:** Preheat the oven to 350°F (175°C). Top the casserole with the remaining shredded cheddar cheese. Bake for 20 minutes or until bubbly and golden.
5. **Serve:** Let it cool slightly before serving.

Chicken Fettuccine Alfredo

Ingredients:

- 2 boneless, skinless chicken breasts
- 1 tbsp olive oil
- 8 oz fettuccine pasta
- 2 tbsp butter
- 1 cup heavy cream
- 1 cup grated Parmesan cheese
- 2 garlic cloves, minced
- Salt and pepper, to taste
- Chopped parsley, for garnish

Instructions:

1. **Cook the Chicken:** Heat olive oil in a skillet over medium heat. Season chicken breasts with salt and pepper and cook for 6-7 minutes per side, until golden and fully cooked. Slice the chicken thinly.
2. **Cook the Pasta:** Boil the fettuccine according to package instructions. Drain and set aside.
3. **Make the Alfredo Sauce:** In the same skillet, melt butter over medium heat. Add garlic and cook for 1 minute. Pour in heavy cream and bring to a simmer. Stir in Parmesan cheese and cook until the sauce thickens, about 3-4 minutes.
4. **Combine:** Add the cooked pasta to the skillet with the sauce. Toss to coat the pasta in the creamy Alfredo sauce. Add the sliced chicken on top.
5. **Serve:** Garnish with chopped parsley and serve immediately.

Chicken and Corn Chowder

Ingredients:

- 2 cups cooked chicken, shredded
- 2 cups frozen corn
- 1 medium onion, chopped
- 2 garlic cloves, minced
- 2 cups chicken broth
- 2 cups heavy cream
- 1 large potato, peeled and diced
- 1 tbsp butter
- 1/2 tsp thyme
- Salt and pepper, to taste
- Chopped green onions, for garnish

Instructions:

1. **Cook the Vegetables:** In a large pot, melt butter over medium heat. Add onion and garlic and cook for 2-3 minutes until softened. Add the diced potato and cook for another 5 minutes.
2. **Simmer the Soup:** Add chicken broth, heavy cream, corn, shredded chicken, thyme, salt, and pepper. Bring to a simmer and cook for 15-20 minutes, until the potatoes are tender.
3. **Blend (Optional):** If you prefer a smoother texture, use an immersion blender to blend part of the soup, leaving some chunks for texture.
4. **Serve:** Ladle the chowder into bowls and garnish with chopped green onions.

Jerk Chicken

Ingredients:

- 4 bone-in chicken thighs
- 1/4 cup olive oil
- 2 tbsp soy sauce
- 1 tbsp brown sugar
- 2 tbsp lime juice
- 1 tbsp grated ginger
- 2 garlic cloves, minced
- 1 tbsp thyme
- 1 tbsp paprika
- 1 tsp ground allspice
- 1 tsp cinnamon
- 1/2 tsp cayenne pepper (optional)
- Salt and pepper, to taste

Instructions:

1. **Make the Marinade:** In a bowl, combine olive oil, soy sauce, brown sugar, lime juice, ginger, garlic, thyme, paprika, allspice, cinnamon, cayenne, salt, and pepper. Mix well.
2. **Marinate the Chicken:** Coat the chicken thighs in the marinade and refrigerate for at least 2 hours, preferably overnight.
3. **Cook the Chicken:** Preheat the grill or oven to medium heat. Grill or bake the chicken for 25-30 minutes, until fully cooked and slightly charred.
4. **Serve:** Serve with rice or vegetables for a complete meal.

Chicken Croquettes

Ingredients:

- 2 cups cooked chicken, shredded
- 1/2 cup breadcrumbs
- 1/4 cup grated Parmesan cheese
- 2 tbsp chopped parsley
- 1/2 tsp garlic powder
- 1 egg, beaten
- 1/4 cup flour
- Salt and pepper, to taste
- Oil for frying

Instructions:

1. **Make the Croquette Mixture:** In a large bowl, combine shredded chicken, breadcrumbs, Parmesan cheese, parsley, garlic powder, egg, flour, salt, and pepper. Mix until fully combined.
2. **Form the Croquettes:** Shape the mixture into small balls or patties.
3. **Fry the Croquettes:** Heat oil in a frying pan over medium heat. Fry the croquettes for 2-3 minutes on each side until golden brown and crispy.
4. **Serve:** Drain on paper towels and serve with dipping sauce, such as ranch or honey mustard.

Chicken Burrito Bowls

Ingredients:

- 2 boneless, skinless chicken breasts
- 1 tbsp olive oil
- 1 tsp cumin
- 1 tsp chili powder
- 1/2 tsp paprika
- 1/2 tsp garlic powder
- 1/2 tsp onion powder
- Salt and pepper, to taste
- 2 cups cooked rice (white or brown)
- 1 cup black beans, drained and rinsed
- 1 cup corn kernels (frozen or fresh)
- 1/2 cup shredded cheese
- 1/2 cup salsa
- 1/4 cup sour cream
- Chopped cilantro, for garnish

Instructions:

1. **Cook the Chicken:** Heat olive oil in a skillet over medium heat. Season the chicken breasts with cumin, chili powder, paprika, garlic powder, onion powder, salt, and pepper. Cook the chicken for 6-7 minutes per side until fully cooked. Slice into strips.
2. **Prepare the Bowl:** In a bowl, layer the rice, black beans, corn, shredded chicken, and cheese.
3. **Top the Bowl:** Spoon salsa and sour cream over the top, then garnish with chopped cilantro.
4. **Serve:** Serve immediately and enjoy a flavorful burrito bowl.

Chicken Tortilla Soup

Ingredients:

- 2 boneless, skinless chicken breasts
- 1 medium onion, chopped
- 2 garlic cloves, minced
- 1 can (14.5 oz) diced tomatoes
- 1 can (4 oz) green chilies
- 4 cups chicken broth
- 1 tsp cumin
- 1 tsp chili powder
- Salt and pepper, to taste
- 1/2 cup corn kernels (frozen or fresh)
- 1/4 cup cilantro, chopped
- Tortilla chips, for topping
- Shredded cheese, for topping
- Sour cream, for topping
- Lime wedges, for serving

Instructions:

1. **Cook the Chicken:** In a large pot, cook chicken breasts in boiling water for 15-20 minutes or until fully cooked. Shred the chicken and set it aside.
2. **Prepare the Soup Base:** In the same pot, sauté chopped onion and garlic in a bit of oil until soft, about 3 minutes. Add diced tomatoes, green chilies, chicken broth, cumin, chili powder, salt, and pepper. Stir well.
3. **Simmer the Soup:** Bring the soup to a boil and then lower to a simmer for 10 minutes.
4. **Add Chicken and Corn:** Add the shredded chicken and corn to the pot. Let it simmer for another 5 minutes.
5. **Serve:** Ladle the soup into bowls, top with crushed tortilla chips, shredded cheese, sour cream, cilantro, and a squeeze of lime juice.

Parmesan Crusted Chicken

Ingredients:

- 4 boneless, skinless chicken breasts
- 1 cup grated Parmesan cheese
- 1 cup panko breadcrumbs
- 2 eggs, beaten
- 1 tbsp olive oil
- Salt and pepper, to taste
- Fresh parsley, chopped (optional)

Instructions:

1. **Preheat the Oven:** Preheat the oven to 400°F (200°C). Line a baking sheet with parchment paper.
2. **Prepare the Coating:** In a shallow dish, combine Parmesan cheese, panko breadcrumbs, salt, and pepper.
3. **Coat the Chicken:** Dip each chicken breast into the beaten eggs, then coat in the Parmesan breadcrumb mixture. Press down to ensure the coating sticks well.
4. **Cook the Chicken:** Heat olive oil in a skillet over medium-high heat. Cook each chicken breast for 2-3 minutes per side until golden brown. Then transfer the chicken to the baking sheet.
5. **Bake:** Bake for 15-20 minutes, or until the chicken reaches an internal temperature of 165°F (74°C).
6. **Serve:** Garnish with fresh parsley and serve with a side of vegetables or salad.

Sweet and Sour Chicken

Ingredients:

- 2 boneless, skinless chicken breasts, cubed
- 1/2 cup cornstarch
- 1 egg, beaten
- 1/4 cup vegetable oil
- 1 bell pepper, chopped
- 1 small onion, chopped
- 1/2 cup pineapple chunks (with juice)
- 1/4 cup soy sauce
- 1/4 cup rice vinegar
- 2 tbsp ketchup
- 1/4 cup brown sugar
- 1/4 tsp garlic powder
- Salt and pepper, to taste

Instructions:

1. **Prepare the Chicken:** Coat the cubed chicken in cornstarch, then dip into the beaten egg.
2. **Fry the Chicken:** Heat vegetable oil in a large pan over medium-high heat. Fry the chicken until golden brown, about 5-7 minutes. Remove from the pan and set aside.
3. **Make the Sauce:** In the same pan, add chopped bell pepper and onion, sauté for 3 minutes. Add pineapple, soy sauce, rice vinegar, ketchup, brown sugar, garlic powder, salt, and pepper. Stir to combine.
4. **Combine the Chicken and Sauce:** Add the fried chicken back into the pan, stirring to coat the chicken in the sweet and sour sauce. Let it simmer for 5 minutes.
5. **Serve:** Serve hot over rice or with noodles.

Mediterranean Chicken Salad

Ingredients:

- 2 boneless, skinless chicken breasts
- 4 cups mixed greens (e.g., spinach, arugula, romaine)
- 1 cucumber, sliced
- 1/2 cup cherry tomatoes, halved
- 1/4 cup Kalamata olives, pitted and sliced
- 1/4 cup red onion, thinly sliced
- 1/4 cup feta cheese, crumbled
- 2 tbsp olive oil
- 1 tbsp lemon juice
- 1 tsp dried oregano
- Salt and pepper, to taste

Instructions:

1. **Cook the Chicken:** Season chicken breasts with salt, pepper, and oregano. Grill or pan-cook the chicken until fully cooked, about 7-8 minutes per side. Let the chicken rest before slicing it.
2. **Prepare the Salad:** In a large bowl, combine mixed greens, cucumber, cherry tomatoes, olives, red onion, and feta cheese.
3. **Make the Dressing:** In a small bowl, whisk together olive oil, lemon juice, dried oregano, salt, and pepper.
4. **Assemble the Salad:** Toss the salad with the dressing. Top with sliced chicken.
5. **Serve:** Serve immediately as a light lunch or dinner.

Chicken Chili

Ingredients:

- 2 boneless, skinless chicken breasts, diced
- 1 medium onion, chopped
- 2 garlic cloves, minced
- 1 can (15 oz) kidney beans, drained and rinsed
- 1 can (15 oz) black beans, drained and rinsed
- 1 can (14.5 oz) diced tomatoes
- 1 can (4 oz) green chilies
- 1 tsp chili powder
- 1/2 tsp cumin
- 1 tsp paprika
- Salt and pepper, to taste
- 2 cups chicken broth
- 1 tbsp olive oil
- Chopped cilantro, for garnish

Instructions:

1. **Cook the Chicken:** Heat olive oil in a large pot over medium heat. Add diced chicken and cook for 5-7 minutes until browned. Remove and set aside.
2. **Cook the Vegetables:** In the same pot, sauté chopped onion and garlic for 2-3 minutes. Add diced tomatoes, green chilies, beans, chicken broth, chili powder, cumin, paprika, salt, and pepper.
3. **Simmer the Chili:** Bring the chili to a boil, then reduce to a simmer. Add the cooked chicken back into the pot. Simmer for 20-25 minutes to combine the flavors.
4. **Serve:** Garnish with chopped cilantro and serve with cornbread or tortilla chips.

Honey Garlic Chicken

Ingredients:

- 4 boneless, skinless chicken thighs
- 2 tbsp olive oil
- 1/4 cup honey
- 2 tbsp soy sauce
- 2 garlic cloves, minced
- 1/2 tsp ground ginger
- Salt and pepper, to taste
- Green onions, for garnish

Instructions:

1. **Cook the Chicken:** Heat olive oil in a skillet over medium heat. Season the chicken thighs with salt and pepper. Cook the chicken for 5-7 minutes on each side until golden brown and cooked through.
2. **Make the Sauce:** In a small bowl, whisk together honey, soy sauce, garlic, and ginger.
3. **Combine the Chicken and Sauce:** Once the chicken is cooked, pour the honey garlic sauce over the chicken in the skillet. Let the sauce simmer for 2-3 minutes, coating the chicken.
4. **Serve:** Garnish with chopped green onions and serve with steamed rice or vegetables.

Chicken Kebabs

Ingredients:

- 2 boneless, skinless chicken breasts, cubed
- 1 bell pepper, cut into chunks
- 1 zucchini, sliced into rounds
- 1 red onion, cut into chunks
- 1/4 cup olive oil
- 1 tbsp lemon juice
- 1 tsp dried oregano
- Salt and pepper, to taste
- Skewers (wooden or metal)

Instructions:

1. **Prepare the Marinade:** In a bowl, mix olive oil, lemon juice, oregano, salt, and pepper. Add chicken cubes and marinate for at least 30 minutes.
2. **Assemble the Kebabs:** Thread chicken, bell pepper, zucchini, and onion onto the skewers.
3. **Grill the Kebabs:** Preheat the grill to medium heat. Grill the kebabs for 8-10 minutes, turning occasionally, until the chicken is fully cooked.
4. **Serve:** Serve the chicken kebabs with a side of rice, couscous, or a fresh salad.